Word Gifts: Keys to Charismatic Power

Fred Lilly

SERVANT BOOKS
Ann Arbor, Michigan

Copyright © 1984 by Fred Lilly

Book Design by John B. Leidy
Cover photo by John B. Leidy © 1984 Servant Publications

Available from Servant Books, Box 8617, Ann Arbor, Michigan 48107

ISBN 0-89283-182-0
Printed in the United States of America

Library of Congress Cataloging in Publication Data

Lilly, Fred.
  Word Gifts.

  Bibliography: p.
  1. Gifts, Spiritual. 2. Christian life — 1960-
I. Title.
BT767.3.L54 1984   234'.13   84-5439
ISBN 0-89283-182-0 (pbk.)

Contents

Introduction / 1
1. God Speaks to His People / 5
2. Wisdom and Knowledge / 13
3. Prophecy / 23
4. Forms of Prophecy / 45
5. Inspired Scripture Readings / 65
6. Responding to the Lord / 71
Suggested Readings / 87

Notes / 91

Introduction

WE ARE PRIVILEGED to live in a century when God is working in dramatic and powerful ways in the lives of millions of people. Among the most remarkable of God's works in our day are the pentecostal and charismatic renewal movements. These movements are distinguished from other Christian movements by their emphasis on the "charismatic gifts of the Holy Spirit" found in St. Paul's first letter to the Corinthians and similar gifts listed in the letter to the Romans and other places in scripture. Through this mighty work of the Holy Spirit, God has brought grace, healing, and power to the Christian people and renewal to his church.

Pentecostal and charismatic renewal emerged first among evangelical Protestants in the first few years after 1900. In the early 1960s the movement spread to members of what are often called the "mainline" Protestant churches—Episcopalians, Presbyterians, Lutherans, and others. In 1967 charismatic renewal came to the Roman Catholic Church when the Lord poured out his Holy Spirit on a small group of college students at Duquesne University in Pittsburgh, Pa. Shortly afterward the renewal spread to the University of Notre Dame and from there to Catholics throughout the world.

Charismatic renewal has borne remarkable spiritual fruit. Many millions of people—Catholics and Protestants, rich and poor, black, white, Hispanic, and Asian—have come into a personal relationship with Jesus Christ and have received the power of the Holy Spirit to live lives of holiness. The charismatic renewal has also led countless non-Christians to a saving encounter with the Lord Jesus.

One of the principal ways charismatic Christians grow spiritually is by banding together in prayer groups to worship the Lord and to hear the word of God. God's word is communicated in three ways during these prayer meetings: through planned teachings, through personal sharings, and through spontaneous exercise of word gifts. Each of these important areas merits a book;

indeed, many such books have been written.

This book is devoted to the word gifts, those scripture-based gifts through which God speaks to a body of Christians. Four basic word gifts—prophecy, wisdom, knowledge and interpretation of tongues—are listed in 1 Corinthians 12:8-11 and are treated more fully by St. Paul in the 13th and 14th chapters of the same letter. This book deals with each of these in some detail. We will also consider another word gift which is commonly experienced at charismatic renewal gatherings—inspired scripture sharing. The gifts of inspired prayer, exhortation, revelation and visions are treated in the chapter on the forms of prophecy.

The chapters that follow draw on my own experiences as a prayer group leader and on the experiences of other prayer group leaders. I have also relied on material published by people who are known and respected as authorities on the gifts of the Holy Spirit. It is my hope and prayer that as more people come to understand and experience the word gifts, God will bless them abundantly with those other precious gifts—the fruit of the Holy Spirit.

This book is written for those who attend

charismatic gatherings, for those who lead them, and for all Christians who believe that God speaks directly to his people. The intention of this book is the same as St. Paul's stated intention in writing the three chapters on gifts to the Christian commuity at Corinth: "Now concerning spiritual gifts, brethren, I do not want you to be uninformed" (1 Cor. 12:11).

I cannot make any claim that this book is an exhaustive treatment of the word gifts. It is, rather, one small volume intended to inform participants in charismatic prayer groups about the word gifts which are being experienced widely by many of their brothers and sisters today. This book is intended to serve as an introduction to the whole area of word gifts. To help the reader study the subject further, a list of suggested books and magazine articles is listed at the end of this volume. The word gifts are keys to charismatic power. The Lord wants to speak to us through them. He wants to use them to renew us in the Holy Spirit. I hope this book will give God's people the desire to seek these mighty gifts of the Spirit.

ONE

God Speaks to His People

IN THE MID-1970s, after I had been leading a small prayer group for some time, I began to study the word gifts of the Holy Spirit. Almost all my Christian friends knew about these gifts and discussed them, but they were not exercised with any regularity in our prayer meetings.

My life had been changed through the charismatic renewal and I had had many charismatic expperiences. I had experienced a number of personal healings; I had listened to inspired teachings, and I had read about other spiritual gifts. I had also been to several charismatic conferences where I had heard prophecies and other inspired words from God.

God had also blessed the prayer group I was leading. Our music ministry was led by a talented professional Christian musician, so our singing was impressive. We had a thriving book ministry, a committed core group, fervent intercessors, and a teaching ministry which had presented Life in the Spirit seminars successfully to several hundred people. We were indeed familiar with the gifts of the Holy Spirit and we had many of the ministries which enable a prayer group to function as an effective "body of Christ."

But even with all these blessings, our group had a major problem: our prayer meetings were flat. They were in a rut. We were not bearing much spiritual fruit. We were not being sufficiently challenged to do things differently.

After a few months of soul-searching by those of us in leadership, the reason became apparent: we were not experiencing the word gifts. We were not seeking them either. We seemed to be guilty of shunning prophecy, of avoiding the words of wisdom and knowledge. We had no experience of interpretation of tongues, inspired prayer, or other verbal messages from God.

Because I was in a position of authority it was my responsibility to seek the Lord for an outpouring of these gifts in our prayer group. I did seek the Lord and he answered.

The Lord's message to me was direct and simple: study the gifts so that you know what they are; learn how to use them yourself; teach others how to use them.

I did all this. I studied about the gifts; I learned how to use them; and I taught others what I had learned. I learned about the gifts by reading articles and by seeking guidance from leaders more mature than myself. What I learned I passed on first to the other members of the core group and then to all the members of the prayer group.

The first few weeks after I taught the prayer group about word gifts I was the only one to exercise them. But gradually others began to exercise them too. Within a few months we were receiving prophecies which provided us with direction and encouragement. Several people began to deliver inspired prayers. In time, wisdom, knowledge, and the other gifts assumed their rightful places in our prayer meetings.

The result in our group was growth, spiritual growth and growth in numbers. Our members began to grow closer to the Lord and closer to one another. We also became better evangelizers. Within a few months, attendance at our prayer meetings grew from around twenty to almost one hundred.

I believe that had we not learned to exercise the word gifts of the Holy Spirit, our prayer group would have dwindled and eventually died out. But we did learn how to seek and exercise the word gifts and literally hundreds of people came to know, love and follow our Lord Jesus Christ as a result.

Father John Randall, pastor of a Catholic church in Providence, Rhode Island and a leader in the charismatic renewal for many years, reports a similar experience with his own prayer group.

Father Randall and others in his parish wanted to attract new people who they thought might not be interested in charismatic renewal. They tried many things. For example, they offered Bible studies with the goal of leading people to a personal commitment to Jesus Christ and, later, to the charismatic renewal.

In 1981, however, Fr. Randall began a "back-to-the-basics" movement. He once again emphasized the spiritual gifts, especially the word gifts. He began to preach and teach about the gifts of the Holy Spirit and to encourage people to attend prayer meetings where the gifts were manifested.

The results were very impressive.

"In August of 1982 we didn't really even have a prayer group," Father Randall said. "By August of 1983 we had over three hundred people coming to weekly prayer meetings to hear God's word."

This new spiritual vitality brought great changes to Fr. Randall's parish. One is a weekly healing service which draws hundreds of people to worship the Lord and pray for his healing.

The experience of my own prayer group and of Father Randall's are not uncommon. Many other prayer groups have had similar experiences. When God's people gather to worship him and hear his word he does wonderful things.

We who want to serve God have an obligation to hear his word. The word gifts are a vitally important way of hearing the Lord. We must take the steps necessary to stir up the word gifts: to encourage and pray for prophecy and interpretation of tongues and wisdom and knowledge.

As we take these steps, God will shower

his blessings upon our groups. He will speak his word and his people will grow accordingly.

The basic scriptural teaching on spiritual gifts is 1 Corinthians 12-14. St. Paul lists the gifts, and then explains how they are to be used by comparing the life of the Christian community with the human body. Both the community and body have many parts, he writes, and each part has a different function. But, every part works with all the other parts for the benefit of the whole.

"To each is given the manifestation of the Spirit for the common good," Paul writes in 1 Cor. 12:7.

Pay close attention to that remarkable statement! The Holy Spirit gives every member of every prayer group spiritual gifts to use to build up others in the group. Each of us should expect spiritual gifts to work in our lives. The purpose of the gifts is to build a body which is strong, vibrant with life, hearing the Lord and responding to his voice. Prayer groups that clearly hear the Lord will have members who love and serve one another, who love and serve the church, and who effectively witness about Christ so that new members enter the body's fellowship regularly.

The Holy Spirit gives spiritual gifts not for the benefit of the individual members alone, but so that together the individuals can grow closer to the Lord and serve him with power.

Now, let us turn to the specific word gifts that we are to seek and exercise.

TWO

Wisdom and Knowledge

ST. PAUL LEADS OFF his list of nine gifts of the Spirit with the gifts of wisdom and knowledge. "To one the Spirit gives wisdom in discourse, to another the power to express knowledge" (1 Cor. 12:8). These are teaching gifts, linked together by Paul because they are closely related.

The gifts of wisdom and knowledge are spiritual gifts. They are different from mere human wisdom and knowledge because they are inspired. The one exercising these gifts is under a special anointing of the Holy Spirit and is well aware of that fact. So are those hearing the message. When the Holy Spirit inspires someone to give a message containing divine wisdom or knowledge, the message goes straight to the heart of those who hear it.

The gift of "wisdom in discourse" refers to

teaching. The gift is, simply stated, a special inspiration to understand a spiritual matter. A person who receives a "word of wisdom" can then give advice to another person or can give a lesson to a Christian assembly—a prayer meeting, for example. God uses the gift of the word of wisdom to teach his people how to live the Christian life.

The word of knowledge is similar. Paul links it with wisdom by presenting it in the same sentence, but he does not explain it as clearly as he explains wisdom. Because of this lack of clarity there are several views among Christians about what this gift really is. Some people, for example, believe that the word of knowledge is a special knowledge of facts about someone that the person receiving the gift could not have otherwise known. Some people even claim to have a "word of knowledge ministry" based on this understanding of the gift.

But others who have studied the scriptures assert that this kind of special knowledge, though a valid gift of the Spirit, is a revelational gift, related to the gift of prophecy. The word of knowledge, they say, is something else.

Two authorities on spiritual gifts, the Assembly of God writer Donald Gee and Stephen Clark, a Roman Catholic, maintain that the word of knowledge is not a revelational gift but a gift of understanding.[1] Clark explains it this way: "The utterance of knowledge . . . is what we would call doctrinal teaching. It is the Spirit inspiring someone to speak an understanding of a truth of the mystery of Christ." The word of knowledge is used in the New Testament "to describe knowledge of God and the mysteries of God," Clark says.

The gifts of wisdom and knowledge often go together. Their purpose is to equip Christians to teach and guide God's people. Knowledge provides information about God; wisdom provides practical ways to put this knowledge to use. St. Paul may have put them at the head of his list of gifts he was recommending to the Corinthians precisely because they are so useful and practical.

The word of wisdom is often manifested in one-on-one situations—when one Christian gives advice to another or when a Christian is sharing the gospel with someone. If we are open to the working of the

Holy Spirit, we will often receive an inspiration about what to say to the person that is just what they need to hear.

This is a significant gift. Quite often we will be talking to someone who has a particular need, or who needs to hear a particular word, in order to turn away from sin or to respond more fully to the Lord's grace. But we often do not know this by our own wisdom, particularly if we do not know the person intimately. In such situations, we should be especially open to the Holy Spirit, amd ask for the gift to know what the person needs to hear.

I have witnessed the word of wisdom in action many times. I once took a friend to a Christian gathering hoping that what he saw and heard would help him make a decision to accept Jesus Christ into his life. After the gathering we got together with one of the leaders—a man who did not know me or my friend. This man told my friend about how many people are kept away from a full life in Christ by fear of losing their freedom.

This was precisely my friend's problem. The fear of losing personal freedom was exactly what was keeping him from accepting Jesus into his life. There was no human way the man we were talking to could have known that, but God knew and he inspired him to give a word of wisdom to my friend. The encounter changed my friend's life and he is a committed Christian today.

The gift works in a similar way in group situations. On one occasion I was speaking to a group of college students who had given their hearts to the Lord but were not making any progress in the Christian life. They had accepted the Lord and had been prayed with for the baptism in the Holy Spirit, but they seemed to have stopped dead in their tracks despite regular attempts at prayer and scripture reading. They didn't know what was the matter and neither did I.

After praying about what to say to these students, I decided to talk about Christian lifestyle. I told them of my own discovery that a life of pleasure-seeking was inconsistent with Christian life. I did not know that many of these students were smoking marijuana and doing other things "for pleasure" that are actually inconsistent with the Christian life. But God knew the needs and inspired me to speak directly about them. He gave me a word of wisdom for this group of people.

Some of these students heeded the message and began seeking the Lord rather than pleasure. Later they told me that they began moving ahead spiritually immediately after deciding to stop doing the pleasure-oriented things they had been doing. The students who didn't heed the message continued to stagnate spiritually and eventually abandoned their efforts to live Christian lives.

Openness to the gifts of wisdom and knowledge in daily Christian living has been called "thinking in the Holy Spirit." We can give our minds over to the Spirit in the same way that we give over our voices and words in order to pray in tongues. When a Christian yields his voice to speak in an unknown tongue, he is speaking in the Spirit; when he seeks God's wisdom before speaking to another he is thinking in the Spirit.

We must not over-spiritualize these things. There is no magical formula to turn on the gifts of wisdom and knowledge at will. We must realize that God works through common sense in most of our dealings with others. But we should be aware that God can inspire us directly to speak his message to a person or a group of persons and we should eagerly seek this gift. Wisdom and knowledge are vitally important and readily available. That is why God gave them to us.

Another way God makes the gift of wisdom available to us is through the wisdom literature of the Bible, especially the books of Wisdom and Proverbs.

These books contain much wisdom that God gave to his people at a particular time and which was recorded for the benefit of subsequent generations. We can turn to any chapter of these books and read the wisdom of God as it was given to someone many centuries ago. When we reflect on these passages today, asking God to apply them to our own lives, they come alive with meaning for us.

I know a woman who was struggling with her role as a Christian wife. She had had a great deal of responsibility in a job before she was married and she was having difficulty adjusting to the role of homemaker after marriage and the birth of three children. One day when she was praying she opened her Bible to the thirty-first chapter of the book of Proverbs. As she read the famous words about the "ideal wife" she began to get a new understanding of the importance and dignity God attaches to this very important role.

This wisdom from God helped this woman see herself and her new role in life in a new way. I think it is accurate to say that God himself gave her a word of wisdom by speaking his word to her through the scripture.

Jesus also uttered words of wisdom many times and some of these are recorded in the gospels. For example, when he told the rich young man to sell all his posessions and follow him (Mark 10:20) he spoke a word of wisdom. There are many other examples in the gospels and in the Acts of the Apostles.

What is the difference between wisdom and knowledge? Donald Gee explains it well in his book on spiritual gifts. "It is helpful to keep in mind," Gee writes, "the well-known and excellent definition of wisdom as 'knowledge rightly applied.' " Gee presents an illustration that brings this more clearly into focus: "I may know that a filling station can provide me with gasoline for my car (knowledge); but it will be wisdom that directs me to fill my tank before commencing on a long journey." Knowledge gives us the facts about the situation; wisdom provides us with the application.

Applying this to Clark's definition of the gifts of wisdom and knowledge we could say the following: The gift of knowledge is divine inspiration of certain facts about God; the gift of wisdom is applying such facts to our daily life, or to the life of another person.

This is exactly what Jesus did in the gospel passages cited above. And this is what happens when we, people filled with the Spirit of Jesus, do when we seek the gifts of wisdom and knowledge. We should seek such gifts before and during prayer meetings, while preparing to give a teaching, when counselling another, and while evangelizing.

THREE

Prophecy

ST. PAUL MENTIONS four word gifts in his first letter to the Corinthians and he encourages Christians to make use of them. One gift, prophecy, is singled out several times as a most useful tool for building up the Christian assembly gathered in prayer.

"Set your hearts on spiritual gifts," Paul writes in 1 Cor. 14:1, "above all, the gift of prophecy...the prophet speaks to men for their upbuilding, their encouragement, their consolation. He who speaks in a tongue builds up himself, but he who prophesies builds up the church."

We who are involved in prayer groups should take St. Paul's exhortation to heart and enthusiastically set about receiving the gift of prophecy. But first, we must understand what this gift is, how prophecies are received, and how prophecy must be tested.

We should also know something about the role of the prophet in the Christian community.

What Is Prophecy?

We will start with a simple explanation of prophecy. Prophecy is a communication from God to an individual or a group of Christians. It is delivered by a person who, under the inspiration of the Holy Spirit, uses his own voice and words to make known the message of God.

In the Old Testament God spoke to his people frequently through prophets. Perhaps the best explanation of the function of prophecy in the Old Testament is found in the conversation between God and Moses in the book of Exodus. In his book *Prophecy*, Bruce Yocum, a recognized prophet himself, explains it this way:

"When God called Moses to take the people of Israel out of Egypt, Moses tried to decline, telling the Lord that he could not speak well enough to talk to the Pharaoh. That excuse didn't help Moses much, however, because God had a solution for the difficulty: Moses' brother Aaron would do the talking:

'When he (Aaron) sees you his heart will be glad. You are to speak with him then, and put the words in his mouth. I will assist both you and him in speaking and will teach the two of you what you are to do. He shall speak to the people for you: he shall be your spokesman, and you shall be as God to him.' (Exod. 4:15-17)

Yocum continues: "In that last line, God makes a direct comparison between the role which Aaron has as Moses' spokesman and the role which a prophet has as God's spokesman....Farther on in the story the Lord says to Moses: 'See! I have made you as God to Pharaoh, and Aaron your brother shall act as your prophet. You shall tell him what I command you. In turn, your brother Aaron shall tell Pharaoh to let the Israelites leave his land. (Exod. 7:1)

"That is the role of the prophet—to be a spokesman for God. A prophet is not a prophet because of what he says, but because of his relationship to God."[1]

This pattern of prophets speaking for God continued throughout the Old Testament. Isaiah, Jeremiah, Exekiel, Haggai, Amos and the other prophets were called by God to speak to his people. Their call was unique because in Old Testament times not all God's people had the same access to the grace of the Holy Spirit.

In the new covenant, the place of prophecy in the life of God's people changed. Gone were the days when only a chosen few could approach the Lord and be his special servants. Because of the new relationship of man to God ushered in by Christ, all who receive Christ are filled with the Holy Spirit, all can directly approach God, all can hear his voice, all can receive gifts for ministry.

But, as we have seen in the letter to the Corinthians, prophecy still plays a major role in the life of God's people. God still uses the prophets and the prophetic gifts to guide his people gathered around him in prayer. Remember, prophecy is a gift for the church, not the individual.

Prophecy was very important in the Christian church for its first 200 years, then it slowly fell into disuse. But it has never completely died out. Many Christian revivals throughout the centuries have been marked by the appearance of charismatic gifts, including the gift of prophecy. This was true of the ascetic movement which led to the formation of many early religious orders; it was true of the Cistercian movement, the Franciscan and Dominican movements, and the "Second Great Awakening" in the United States in the nineteenth Century.

Today's charismatic renewal is another Christian movement which benefits greatly from God's generous outpouring of the gift of prophecy and the other charismatic gifts.

What exactly are prophecies? We have already seen that it is a gift through which God speaks to a body of Christians gathered around him in prayer. What kinds of messages does he speak? We will answer this question by looking first at the scriptures and then at contemporary charismatic renewal experience.

Prophecy was, of course, a key element of God's dealing with his people in Old Testament days. Through the prophets, God told his people what he expected of them. He used the prophets to call his people to repentance and to comfort them when they were oppressed. He also used prophecy to instruct them about the coming of the One who was to set all people free for all eternity.

The New Testament is also filled with examples of prophecy. The Acts of the Apostles records at least five examples of prophetic activity. The other books of the New Testament record many more.

The instances of prophetic activity in Acts are varied and show how useful to Christians this gift is. For example, in Acts 11 a prophet named Agabus predicted that a famine would soon come upon the Roman world. That famine did indeed occur and the prophecy of Agabus enabled the Christians to prepare for it.

Another example: in Acts 13 we read about the leaders of the church at Antioch gathered in prayer. While they were praying a prophetic instruction was received: God wanted Paul and Barnabas to depart on a missionary journey. In Acts 15 we read about how the prophets Judas and Silas encouraged and strengthened the church at Antioch through a prophetic utterance.

Prophecy was important from the earliest days of the church, and it is important in the Pentecostal and charismatic renewal movements. This is appropriate because of the importance St. Paul places on it and because of its history in guiding Christian renewal movements throughout the ages.

Prophecy is an important part of the prayer meetings and charismatic conferences. The Lord has used this gift to teach us many things and to form us into a people who are capable of following him. Two examples are particularly revealing.

A few years ago a group of leaders of prayer groups began discussing the importance of the groups in their region joining together regularly for common teaching and fellowship. This idea was controversial because many prayer group leaders thought such a move might threaten the existence of their prayer groups. So the idea was taken to the Lord during a leaders' prayer day. Many leaders had a strong sense that the Lord did indeed want the groups to join together. Their sense was confirmed by a prophetic utterance which called the leaders to band themselves together.

A more well-known example of the importance of prophecy are what have come to be called the "Rome prophecies." These were two prophecies delivered in St. Peter's Basilica during the 1975 International Catholic Charismatic Conference in Rome. The prophecies spoke of "hard times" approaching for the church and the world and called on those present to draw even closer to the Lord.

The charismatic renewal experienced some dramatic changes after these Rome prophecies. Prayer groups began banding together for mutual support. Some prayer groups merged with more mature ones and in some places entire prayer communities moved from one location to another. Hundreds of people actually gave up jobs and homes and moved thousands of miles to be part of a more mature body of Christians.

In other places, Christians responded to the Rome prophecies by dedicating themselves to intercession and fasting for God's mercy and strength. Many people have indeed experienced the "hard times" as prophesied. But they were prepared because God had spoken to them to prepare them and strengthen them.

These examples of prophecy in action show how varied are the messages God gives his people through the exercise of this gift. Indeed, scripture and charismatic renewal experience show that prophecy has four purposes:

1. Encouragement: Perhaps the most common prophecies are those that "encourage and strengthen" us (see Acts 15:32 and

1 Cor. 14:3). Prophecies of this type revive our spirits when we are dejected, give us hope when we are discouraged, and strengthen us when we feel weak or tired.

2. *Reproof*: From time to time the Holy Spirit will rebuke either an individual or a group of Christians through prophecy. God's purpose in these cases is to call our attention to our sin or to correct us when we have strayed from his purposes for us. This kind of prophecy has a positive purpose: it helps us seek Christ's freedom from the tyranny of sin and it enables us to return to the Lord's ways which bring joy and peace.

3. *Inspiration*: Inspirational prophecies are those that draw us closer to God in worship. In these cases the spirit of adoration promoted by the prophecy is much more important than the words; God is trying to *do* something to us rather than say something to us.

4. *Guidance*: Prophecies which give God's people clear direction and guidance can be found throughout the scriptures and are also common in the charismatic renewal today. Some of these prophetic gifts are for general guidance, such as revelations about God's

general plan of salvation. But at other times these prophecies are very specific (see Jer. 28.16 and Acts 11:27 ff).

A more recent example of such specific directional prophesy was shared by Demos Shakarian, a founder of the Full Gospel Business Men's Fellowship. I heard him tell this story during a television interview.

Shakarian related the story of his grandparents, an Armenian couple, parents of five daughters. Apparently it was considered a great disgrace for an Armenian couple not to have a son. But one day, May 25, 1891 to be exact, a relative, who was also a pentecostal Christian, told Shakarian's grandmother that he had a word from the Lord for her. He prophesied that one year from that day she would give birth to a son.

Sure enough, exactly one year later, the woman gave birth to a son. The joyous couple named their baby Isaac, for he was the fruit of a fulfilled promise of God, just as was the son of Abraham.

The Prophet

Now that we have seen some of the ways God speaks to his people in prophecy, what about the prophet? How does the prophet speak the word of the Lord?

In both the Old and New Testaments prophets saw themselves as messengers of God, authorized by God to bring his word to his people. The messages were different and the styles varied. But the nature of prophecy itself was always the same—God was speaking a message to his people through a messenger he appointed from their midst.

This is true also of prophecy and prophets in prayer groups today. God calls forth the gift of prophecy and entrusts to a very few the actual office of prophet. Bruce Yocum writes perceptively about prophets:

"Not all of those who prophesy are prophets. Paul says in 1 Corinthians 14 that all can prophesy (v.31), but he also asks 'Are all prophets?' and the answer is 'no.' Paul speaks of both 'spirituals' and of 'gifts of the spirit' and the two are not the same. A 'spiritual' is a manifestation—a breaking forth—of the power of the Holy Spirit in prophecy (or in healing, working a miracle, etc.). A 'gift of the Holy Spirit' is the equipment which fits an individual to take his particular role among God's people. In other words, Paul says that many can prophesy by a 'working of the Holy Spirit,' but that only some have the 'gift' to be a prophet."[2]

The leaders of a prayer group have the very serious responsibility of determining who, if anyone, is to function as a prophet. This is not a matter of choosing a likely candidate and praying for the Lord to give this person the gift. Rather, it is a matter of discernment, of examining those people in the prayer group who do receive prophecies to see if the Lord has actually appointed one or more of them to be prophets. Again I emphasize that this is very rare and such determinations can only be made after much discernment. There are two things to look for when making such an examination.

1. The candidate's personal life. In order for a person to serve God in any capacity of responsibility in a prayer group, that person must be emotionally stable and must lead a strong and consistent Christian life. It is true that God can heal any problem in any of these areas, but that healing must be given time to really take root and stabilize a person's life before that person tries to function in any leadership role. Since a prophet is a leader of God's people, these personal qualities of stability and maturity are very important.

2. *Manifestation of spiritual gifts.* In a prayer group, many people will manifest true prophetic gifts, but some will do so with more power and greater results than others. A person who consistently expresses prophecies which are powerful and which change the lives of many in the group can be considered to have a prophetic gift.

Yocum lists the following as the "primary characteristics of an abiding prophetic gift": an ongoing and consistent exercise of prophecy over a period of four or five years; a powerful and effective exercise of prophetic gifts which consistently change people and move the community forward in God's purpose; ability to "stir up" the gift (can be counted on to deliver a true prophecy when the community needs to hear from God); and, a true gift of revelation which operates consistently.[3]

Yocum's last characteristic—consistent revelation—introduces a new term.

Revelation is the act of making known things which have been hidden. A good example is God's revelation to the prophet

Nathan of King David's sin with Bathsheba. In a prayer group, a revelation would more typically be on the order of opening the eyes of people in the group to things which may be blocking spiritual progress, or revealing the depth of the love God has for the members of the group, or knowledge of a spontaneous healing in a person present at a meeting.

A prayer group should not be too eager to decide that a particular person is truly a prophet. As we have seen, prophecy is serious business and those who hold the office of prophet are actually rare. A person must manifest a variety of prophetic gifts in a responsible and consistent manner for many years before that person can truly be considered a prophet.

However, a prayer group should not shy away from seeking prophecies simply because a person with a tested and discerned gift of prophecy is not available. The Lord has given manifestations of prophecy to charismatic prayer groups countless times. Prophecy is a normal part of prayer group activity; it should be sought on a regular basis.

Delivering Prophecy

Let us now briefly examine what we might well call the "technical aspects" of prophecy: how a prophecy is received and how it should be expressed. We will also consider how leaders should test prophecy.

Prophecies come to people as they place themselves in the presence of the Lord, worshipping him and opening themselves to receive his word. They can be received when a person is praying alone or within a larger body of Christians.

Prophecies typically come to people in three ways. Sometimes a person receives an entire prophetic message, every single word. At other times he or she will receive a clear sense of only the first few words, along with a more general sense of a message that God wants to be delivered in a prophetic form. Sometimes the prophet will receive only the sense of the prophecy—that is, the idea God wants to communicate rather than specific words.

The word "anointing" is often used in connection with prophecy. This word comes from the Old Testament practice of anointing a person or an object with oil during a ceremony of dedication to God. When people speak of anointing today they usually mean the action of the Holy Spirit as he prepares a person to exercise some spiritual gift.

We can speak of a person receiving an anointing to prophesy. What this means is that a person in prayer has an experience of God giving them a prophetic message to share with others. Sometimes this inner conviction is accompanied by feelings such as excitement. Sometimes he or she will not experience any particular emotion.

The important thing to remember when experiencing such inner conviction is that prophecy is serious: the person should prophesy only when he or she is certain that the message is from God and God has authorized the person to speak it. Giving a message that is not truly "anointed" is a serious matter. Failing to give a prophetic message that God has indeed anointed is also a serious matter. In all cases, we must remember to be faithful to the Spirit's promptings so that God's intentions are honored.

Since the Lord uses an individual as his vehicle of communication, the words of the prophecy will be consistent with the way that person speaks. For instance, people whose churches use the King James version of the Bible will often prophesy in that Bible's archaic English. Or a person who regularly uses a lot of very descriptive words in normal language will often use a lot of those kinds of words in a prophecy.

The language a person uses in a prophecy is indeed under that person's control. As a matter of fact, a person uttering a prophecy is responsible for the language of that prophecy. This means the person prophesying has a responsibility to speak the prophesy in words that people can understand.

The same principle holds true for manner of delivery. An extroverted person will prophesy in a way consistent with his personality. A quiet person will prophesy differently. But each has a responsibility to make certain that the style of delivery of the prophetic word is appropriate for the prophesy. Normally, this means delivering the prophecy in a simple, straightforward way, speaking loudly enough so everyone present can hear, and avoiding unnecessary drama.

Prophecies must also be delivered in the right place at the right time. Prayer meetings usually have particular times during which word gifts are appropriate. Usually this is during the first half of a meeting when those present are worshipping God and awaiting his word. Right after the conclusion of a teaching or during announcements are not appropriate times to prophesy. Prophesying during church services is not appropriate unless word gifts are a normal part of the service. Likewise, at many charismatic conferences "word gift groups" are organized for the exercise of prophecy and other word gifts. It is not appropriate for a person not in the word gift group to attempt to prophesy from his seat, unless such an action has been encouraged by those responsible for leading the conference.

Some people argue that placing these kinds of restrictions on the exercise of prophetic gifts stifles the Holy Spirit. Actually these few simple guidelines are in keeping with St. Paul's instruction to exercise the gifts "properly and in order" (see 1 Cor. 14:40).

Testing Prophecy

Because prophecy is such a powerful word gift, Christians have a serious responsibility to test and discern it. How should we do this?

We know from biblical history and from Christian history that false prophecy has caused many problems for God's people (see Kings, chapter 22 and Jer. 28). Jesus also warned us to beware of false prophets (see Matt. 7:15 and 24:24). We should beware of them today. Leaders in particular have a responsibility to make certain that any word gift exercised within the group is consistent with God's revelation through scripture and the teaching of the church.

At the same time, such testing requires wisdom and the ability to discern because we don't want to be in a position of choking off God's word in order to guard against abuses. St. Paul was very clear about that point: "Do not stifle the Spirit. Do not despise prophecies. Test everything; retain what is good" (1 Thess. 5:19-21). Following are five guidelines for testing prophecy.

1. The life of the prophet. Jesus spoke about distinguishing good fruit from bad fruit as the test of a person (see Luke 6:43-44). This applies to prophecy in an obvious way. If the person who gives a particular prophecy lives a mature, stable, consistent Christian life, he or she can be trusted as a prophet. A person whose life is not in proper order emotionally and spiritually cannot be as easily trusted. We should never accept "prophecies" from people who are not Christians.

2. Testing the message. The most important test of a prophetic message is consistency with Christian revelation. God has told us everything we need to know for salvation and personal growth through the Bible and the teaching of our church. Any prophetic message must be consistent with this revelation. We must also be able to understand the message. If a message is mysterious or hard to grasp, it probably is not prophecy but rather the product of someone's imagination. This does not necessarily mean the message is untrue; it means that it is not prohecy.

3. Testing the spirits. Testing the message only tells us if the message is consistent with Christian truth; it does not tell us that the message is really prophecy. To make this determination, we must find out if the message is really inspired by the Holy Spirit. This is not a difficult matter for someone who has a mature relationship with the Lord, because such a person knows well the voice of his Lord. When a true prophecy is spoken, our hearts and our spirits will respond to it.

Another aspect of judging the spirits is judging the tone of the prophecy. The Holy Spirit is our comforter and our guide, he does not frighten or condemn us. Therefore, messages which are frightening or excessively gloomy are probably not really prophecies. This does not mean all prophecy must have a "positive message." We have seen how the Lord corrects us and even tells us about our sin through prophecy. But he will do this in a way that reassures us of his help. We must, of course, use common sense in making such judgments rather than relying on feelings. A particular prophecy can move us to remorse, as Nathan's prophecy moved King David (2 Sam 12), and still be a positive message of God's salvation.

Another very important aspect of testing the spirits is to determine if the message glorifies our Lord Jesus Christ. If prophetic messages do not lead us to worship and thanksgiving, we can be sure they are not from the Holy Spirit.

4. Does it bear fruit? A true word from God will bear good fruit. It will lead us to repentance, worship, or renewed commitment to service in Christ's body. By paying attention to such fruit, we can not only test the authenticity of a prophetic gift, but also the degree to which a person is gifted with prophecy.

5. Does it really happen? In the case of prophecy predicting a particular happening, we know that if the event does not occur, the message was not prophecy. But, even if the event does occur, we still must apply the other tests of prophecy because even false prophets can sometimes accurately predict future events (see Deut. 13:1-3).

Thus far we have discussed prophecy as if the typical prayer meeting prophecy were the only way the gift is exercised. Actually the prophetic gift has several forms, all found in scripture and all experienced, at least occasionally, by many charismatic prayer groups. Each of these forms of prophecy is discussed in the next chapter.

FOUR

Forms of Prophecy

We have seen how God speaks to his people through manifestations of prophecy and through the gift of prophecy which he bestows on certain persons. Prophecy is actually a gift which takes many forms. These are found in scripture and are experienced widely among today's charismatic renewal prayer groups.

The forms of prophecy are: prophetic oracles, prophetic exhortation, inspired prayer, prophecy in song, revelation, personal prophecy, prophecy in personal prayer, visions, prophetic actions, and interpretation of tongues. In the remainder of this chapter, each of these is explained briefly and illustrated with examples from recent charismatic renewal gatherings or from scripture.

Oracles

Prophetic oracles are brief, direct prophetic communications to God's people, usually delivered in the first person as if God himself were speaking. Oracles are very common and very useful because they are simple statements of what God wants his people to hear. Oracles often begin with a phrase such as "thus says the Lord" or "hear me my people." This is not a requirement, of course, but it is a common experience.

Oracles are what people usually think of when they hear the word "prophecy." This form of the gift is common at charismatic prayer meetings and conferences. It is probably not the most frequently manifested form of prophecy, but it is most closely associated with the gift because these messages are usually brief and easy to remember and because of the bold proclamation of the prophet: this is the word of the Lord to us.

An example of a prophetic oracle, delivered at a recent national charismatic conference, is:

"My people, do not think you are too small to be my witnesses. Do not think you are too little to be used by me. I used David, a shepherd boy. I used Mary, a Jewish maiden. I used fishermen and tax collectors. I used soldiers and slaves. Those I called I empowered to do what I called them to do. Be my witnesses, in little places and in great. Be my witnesses wherever you are."[1]

Prophetic Exhortation

The New Testament phrase "exhortation" is often rendered in modern English as "encouragement." So a prophetic exhortation is a word from God which encourages — revives, renews, or strengthens his people. Bruce Yocum says that exhortation is probably the most common form of prophecy. It is indeed useful because with all the struggles we human beings go through in our lives, we need the Lord's encouragement frequently; our spiritual lives need to be revived and renewed from time to time and we need strength to live for God on a daily basis.

Many times during prayer meetings people will share an encouraging word. Personal sharings are often encouraging; a "pep talk" from a brother or a sister can revive us and renew us. But these are not always prophetic exhortations. Prophecy is inspired by the Holy Spirit in a way that a personal opinion or a testimony is not. A personal sharing or opinion comes out of that person's experience and may even be inspired, but it is not prophecy. A prophetic exhortation comes directly from the Lord; you might say it is the "Lord's opinion," rather than that of the person throught whom the message comes.

An example of a prophetic exhortation which was received with great joy by those who heard it because it was so encouraging, was delivered several years ago at another national charismatic conference:

"You can know in joy that my Holy Spirit is upon you, and that my presence is with you in the time of testing that lies ahead; for when you are called to suffer in the days to come, to spend yourselves in the days to come, to lay down your lives, your homes, your money—there are even some among you who will shed your blood for my name's sake—when that day comes you will say that I spoke to you on this night, and showed you my presence and my power. . . ."[2]

Inspired Prayer

Frequently in a prayer meeting someone will pray aloud in a way that is profoundly moving for all present. This is usually the manifestation of inspired prayer. Sometimes this prayer will even contain elements of prophetic revelation—foretelling some sort of spriritual event which will occur among the people present. The prayer of Zechariah and Simeon in the first and second chapters of Luke are examples of this kind of inspired prayer.

Inspired prayer is a useful gift, common among charismatic prayer groups. It often will be used by God to open a prayer meeting by calling those present to profound worship; or it will be given at the close of a meeting, to send the community off to love and serve the Lord.

The prayer of the apostles in Acts chapter four is a good example of inspired prayer:

"Sovereign Lord, who made heaven and earth and sea and all that is in them, You have said by the Holy Spirit through the lips of our father David your servant:

'Why did the Gentiles rage, the peoples conspire in folly? The kings of the earth were aligned, the princes gathered together against the Lord and against his anointed.'

"Indeed, they gathered in the very city against your holy Servant, Jesus, whom you anointed—Herod and Pontius Pilate in league with the Gentiles and the peoples of Israel. They have brought about the very things which in your powerful providence you planned long ago. But now, O Lord, look at the threat they are leveling against us. Grant to your servants, even as they speak your words, complete assurance by stretching forth your hand in cures and signs and wonders to be worked in the name of Jesus, your holy Servant." (Acts 4:24-30)

The scripture tells us that as the apostles prayed that prayer, the building they were in shook, they were all filled with the power of the Holy Spirit and continued to speak God's word to the people of Jerusalem with boldness and confidence.

Although most modern manifestations of inspired prayer do not have such dramatic effects, they are profoundly moving and bear great fruit by setting the men and women present on fire for the Lord. God indeed uses this gift to build up his people.

Prophecy in Song

This is, obviously, the utterance of prophecy in the form of a song. Such a prophecy is usually chanted or sung to an inspired melody. Typically, this kind of prophecy is a song in praise of God's majesty or his goodness and serves as a call to worship. Sometimes a prophetic message is delivered through song.

Prophecy in song is very inspiring and people who have good voices and have received manifestations of prophecy should be open to prophesying this way. A song prophecy is received in a similar way as other prophecies. Sometimes it will start with a simple message and a melody or chant will also be received. At other times the person receives only the words to the prophecy but also feels an urge to sing it rather than speak it. Prayer groups which are accustomed to prophecy should try to "stir up" the gift of prophetic song among those members who receive prophecies—a deepening of the group's worship is the typical result.

Revelation

The scriptures—both the Old and New Testaments—are filled with episodes of prophets foretelling a future event or revealing things about other people which they would not ordinarily have known. This gift of prophetic revelation served God's purposes among his people in Bible days and manifestations of the gift are not unusual today.

Prophetic revelation is one area where great caution is essential. Many people who have claimed to possess this kind of special knowledge have many times been wrong and have done great harm to Christianity. It is possible for a person to be mistaken, to believe they have received a revelation when they actually have not. Another area of caution is that sometimes, even when a revelation is genuine, it is not always appropriate to let others know about it.

But, even with these cautions in mind, we need to be as open to this type of prophecy as to any other. It is after all a gift God has given for our use. St. Paul went so far as to tell the Christians of Corinth that God has a special purpose for this gift: "If all prophesy, and an unbeliever or outsider enters, he is convicted by all, he is called to account by all; the secrets of his heart are disclosed; and so, falling on his face, he will worship God and declare that God is really among you." (1 Cor. 14:24-25)

Perhaps the best example of the manifestation of this gift occured when Jesus went to get a drink of water at a well: "He (Jesus) said to her, 'Go, call your husband, and then come back here.' 'I have no husband,' replied the woman. 'You are right in saying you have no husband!' Jesus exclaimed. 'The fact is, you have had five, and the man you are living with now is not your husband. What you said is true.'

" 'Sir,' answered the woman, 'I can see you are a prophet.' " (John 4:16-19)

Jesus revealed something which was hidden, and which he had no knowledge of because he did not know the woman. She had no doubt what had taken place: she knew he had a prophetic gift and told him so. This episode also shows one of the purposes of prophecy in action. Jesus' prophecy convicted the woman of her sin; he explained her sin to her and offered her God's eternal promise of forgiveness.

Personal Prophecy

The Lord can, and often does, speak to individuals as well as to groups through prophetic gifts. The prophecy of Agabus to Paul (see Acts 21:10ff) and of Nathan to King David (see 2 Sam. 12) are manifestations of this kind of prophetic utterance. So too today God speaks to individuals through prophecy.

I know a man who occasionally receives prophetic messages for other people during his daily prayer time. On one occasion he was praying for a friend who was going through a difficult time in his Christian life, a time of doubt that at times bordered on despair. While the man was praying for his friend he sensed that he had a message for him from the Lord.

The prophetic message itself was very simple. The Lord wanted the man to know that he (God) loved him very much and that he was indeed active in his life. The prophetic word went on to say that the time of trial was nearing its end and that the man would emerge from it a more mature Christian.

The man went to his friend and told him that he believed he had a message from God for him. The friend received the news with joy because the Lord had been preparing him to receive a consoling and encouraging word. This prophecy was fulfilled shortly afterwards and the man who received consolation from it has shared many times with his friend how instrumental this word from the Lord was in enabling him to grow closer to the Lord.

Personal prophecy can be misused. People can claim to have received a prophecy simply to get their own way. One leader told me that he knows of a case in which one person prophesied to another that "the Lord wanted them to get married." It is obvious that such personal prophecies need to be discerned and judged by mature pastoral leaders before they are acted upon.

Prophecy in Personal Prayer

It is possible for a person to receive a prophetic word from God while they are praying alone. Sometimes this is a word for the person alone; and sometimes it is being given for sharing at a later gathering of a Christian assembly.

Caution is vital if the personal prophecy is for the individual. Since there is not a group of Christian people around to discern the prophecy, it cannot be relied on for guidance. Indeed, personal prophecies usually are words of comfort and encouragement from a loving Father, often coming at times of emotional or spiritual need.

I once experienced such a prophecy. Shortly after being baptized in the Holy Spirit and beginning to experience all the heightened spiritual sensitivities that followed, I became extremely remorseful for my past sins and I worried a great deal about my own weaknesses. I was beginning to convince myself that I would have a very hard time receiving God's gift of eternal salvation because I had so many weaknesses and fell so easily into sin.

One evening I told all this to the good friend who had instructed me in the ways of the Lord and had prayed with me for the baptism in the Holy Spirit. He said many truthful things about God's mercy and love, but I still was not convinced. Later that evening while I was praying alone, I received a very clear word from the Lord, a true prophecy. This is what it took to convince me that God was indeed powerful and merciful enough to strengthen even the likes of me against my sinful tendencies.

I don't remember receiving such a prophecy again, even though I have experienced the Lord speaking to me many times since then. I believe that prophecy in personal prayer is relatively rare. But that does not mean they do not occur. God is sovereign, after all!

Visions

Visions are another common form of prophecy. Examples from scripture include many passages in the book of Revelation. The prophet Ezekiel also experienced many visions. Today, God uses this gift to instruct and edify his people.

One time, when our prayer group was at a significant turning point in its development, the Lord spoke to us through a prophetic vision. A member of our group, one who had been used by God to speak many times through prophecy, had a vision during her personal prayer time. She told the leaders about it and we had a chance to decide if it was truly word from the Lord to us. While we prayed we received many confirmations that indeed this vision was the Lord's word. Such discernment is absolutely necessary in judging the appropriateness of publicly sharing visions.

At the time, our prayer group had been growing rather rapidly (the result of learning how to use word gifts, as I explained earlier) and we were developing a number of new ministries and services. We who were leaders were seeking wisdom from the Lord so we could care for the people he was adding to our group. We were trying to teach all our members that being firmly rooted in faith with a personal relationship with Jesus was the vital element to sustain them while they were learning how to balance all the complicated elements of day-to-day Christian life. We also knew this to be absolutely necessary for our group as a whole.

The vision gave us a concrete model to apply this wisdom. Our sister saw a great tree. Its many branches represented the different elements in daily life: family responsibilities, work, exercise, personal prayer, scripture reading, service to parish and prayer group, and on and on. The trunk of the tree, which connected all these elements of a person's daily life to its roots, was the body of Christ—both the prayer group and the church. The roots, which drew nourishment from the soil, were the various activities of the prayer group and the church: prayer, teaching, liturgy, service, fellowship. The soil, which was seen as "living earth and water," was God's grace.

This vision may not sound very profound in the retelling, but it was a breakthrough for several dozen people in our prayer group. We had been teaching about all the things in the vision. We had even shown people diagrams and drawings that said the same things. But this vision was a word from God for us. Our Father had spoken directly to us to clear up our confusion about how best to serve him. Our growth in holiness and service took a great stride forward the day this vision and a teaching based on it were presented to our prayer group.

Prophetic Actions

Sometimes the Lord inspires actions to accompany prophecies. We see this in both the Old and New Testaments (see Jer. 27:2-3 and Acts 21:10-11). Prophetic actions dramatize God's message to his people in a way that words alone sometimes cannot. The prophets of the Bible did not engage in prophetic actions because they thought it added a nice touch to their prophesying. They did it because God inspired them to do it. We have to be very careful to be certain we are not doing prophetic actions for dramatic effect, but only because God inspires them.

Interpretation of Tongues

St. Paul listed intrepretation of tongues separate from prophecy in his list of gifts in the first letter to the Corinthians. But later, in 1 Cor. 14, he linked the two together. It is clear from the latter that interpretation of tongues is a manifestation of the gift of prophecy.

Here's what St. Paul had to say: "I should like it if all of you spoke in tongues, but I much prefer that you prophesy. The prophet is greater than one who speaks in tongues, unless the speaker can also interpret for the upbuilding of the church....This means that the man who speaks in a tongue should pray for the gift of interpretation." (1 Cor. 14:5, 13)

What St. Paul is saying here is that like prophecy, interpretation of tongues builds up those who hear it. As a matter of fact, a prophecy in tongues with an interpretation in the language of the people present is a very dramatic way for God to communicate with his people. This is a gift that should be experienced often in prayer groups, but it should be done in good order, as St. Paul instructed the Christians of Corinth:

"If any speak in a tongue, let there be two or at most three, and each in turn; and let one interpret. But if there is no one to interpret, let each of them keep silence in the assembly and speak to himself and to God." (1 Cor. 14:27-28)

It is important to keep one thing about these passages in mind: St. Paul was referring to word gift messages in tongues, not to prayer tongues that are often spoken or sung during times of worship in prayer meetings. Prayer tongues are for praise and do not require an interpretation because, as St. Paul says in the same passage, we are talking to God, not to men.

Interpretation of tongues is inspired the same way as any prophecy. The difference is that when the person feels the "anointing" to prophesy, the message is in an unknown tongue rather than that person's language. Often, that person will also receive an interpretation of the inspired message, that is, the same message of the tongue only in the language spoken by the people at the prayer meeting. On other occasions, a person will be inspired to speak a message in tongues and another will receive the interpretation.

Certainly the most dramatic example of interpretation of tongues was the experience of the apostles on the day of Pentecost. God inspired them to boldly proclaim a message to people on the streets of Jerusalem. They spoke in languages they had not learned and God performed a mighty act of interpretation: people understood what was being said even if they did not know the language being spoken. The result was several thousand conversions. God had used a certain manifestation of the gift of tongues to draw attention to his message of salvation.

Many people today have a similar experience of tongues and interpretation. This unique "grace of Pentecost," which first appeared on the day the Holy Spirit came upon the disciples of Jesus, still today draws the attention of people in prayer meetings. God still uses it to speak to those he is forming into his body. Some of the most dramatic messages of God to his people have been manifestations of interpretation of tongues.

For example, at a recent conference for prayer group leaders at the University of Steubenville in Ohio the Lord spoke repeatedly through prophecy, scripture and teaching about the fire of the Holy Spirit. The Lord was teaching these leaders to rely on him more than they ever have; and he was showing them that he was preparing them for powerful service of his people. This was confirmed by several prophecies and by the following interpretation of tongues:

"The Lord says: I am in your midst as your shepherd. I have gathered you together as my flock. The Lord says: I am in your midst as your healer and I desire to heal the wounded. I am in your midst as your Father, the one who cares for you, loves you. Come to me, come to me, and you will rest. Come to me and you will find power. Come to me and you will find strength for your life. For I am in your midst as a consuming fire. I will burn out what is within you that I do not desire, and I will empower you with the power of my love to serve me. Come to me; I am in your midst and I am your Lord."

At the conclusion of this word from God many of the people attending that conference fell to their knees as a sign of acceptance of God's will. This is precisely the attitude all God's people should have when we hear his word. We should prostrate our hearts before him. We should indicate to God our willingness to obey his word. We should express to him our thankfulness that he speaks his mind to us.

FIVE

Inspired Scripture Readings

OPEN THE NEW TESTAMENT at random to almost any page of any epistle and you will find a reference, if not a direct quote, from another book of scripture. The use of scripture passages to convey a message from God to mankind began in scripture itself.

Similarly, Christians have been taking advantage of the written word of God to instruct other Christians down through the centuries. St. Paul made numerous references to the Hebrew scriptures—our Old Testament—in his Epistles. Other great teachers, from the Fathers of the early church to the charismatic renewal teachers of today, have used both the Old and New Testaments in teaching.

The use of inspired scripture passages during prayer meetings is perhaps the most common of the word gifts experienced by charismatic prayer groups today. The Lord used his own written word to speak particular messages to a body of believers gathered around him in prayer. Even though the use of inspired scripture passages is not specifically mentioned in St. Paul's list of charismatic gifts, it clearly ranks with prophecy, wisdom and knowledge as an inspired and commonly manifested word gift.

Scripture itself attests to the value of the written word of God: "Likewise, from your infancy you have known the sacred Scriptures, the source of the wisdom which through faith in Jesus Christ leads to salvation. All scripture is inspired of God and is useful for teaching—for reproof, correction, and training in holiness so that the man of God may be fully competent and equipped for every good work." (2 Tim. 15-17)

When he wrote those words to his disciple Timothy, St. Paul was attributing great value to the wisdom of the Hebrew scriptures which, coupled with faith in Jesus Christ, leads to salvation. Christians today have access to the even more valuable wisdom of the New Testament, the testimony of the early Christians to Jesus Christ, our savior and our Lord. Just as Timothy could turn to his scriptures for wisdom, reproof, correction and training in holiness, so can we turn to the scriptures—Old and New Testaments. Like Timothy, that great pioneer in our faith, we too can become "fully competent" in the Christian life and "equipped for every good work" by receiving and obeying God's word as revealed through the scriptures.

An inspired scripture passage is received just like any other word gift. A person in conversation with the Lord in prayer receives an inspiration, an "anointing," to turn to a particular scripture passage. Sometimes the passage is well known to the person; sometimes it may be newly encountered or understood in a new way.

Often, the inspired passage is intended by the Lord to instruct only the person who reads the passage. For example, the person may be feeling disappointed or somewhat depressed and turn to the gospel passage where Jesus says "cast your burdens upon me."

At other times the Holy Spirit's intention in calling a particular scripture passage to mind is that the passage be read aloud for the edification of the assembly. Sometimes the passage will be a psalm or a section from an epistle which proclaims God's goodness and calls the assembly into a deeper sense of worship. At other times the passage will be in response to a prophecy or word of wisdom; it will confirm or shed additional light on the message of the earlier gift.

It is important that every prayer group participant keep this distinction in mind: not every inspired scripture passage is to be read aloud, but many are. The individual receiving the passage should be attentive to the Holy Spirit. Ask him in prayer who the passage is meant for. Try to determine if the passage really fits with what the Lord is saying at the particular meeting. As a person makes use of this gift and heeds the Spirit's voice, discernment becomes easier.

A typical prayer meeting might contain as few as two or three or as many as a dozen inspired scripture passages. Often, a prayer meeting starts with the leader reading a scripture passage he received while praying for the meeting. The first portion of most prayer meetings is devoted to praise and worship and usually several scripture passages are shared during such a time. These passages tend to deepen the sense of worship or convey messages from the Lord to the assembly.

The proper time for word gift manifestation is usually towards the end of the initial time of worship. And inspired scripture passages are normally shared during such times of word gift manifestations.

Often too, a time of worsip and a prayer meeting itself is closed with a scripture reading that tops off or summarizes what has been said during the meeting. And many a personal sharing or testimony by a brother or sister is amplified by one or more inspired reference to the word of God.

It is clear from these examples how versatile and valuable is the gift of inspired scripture passages. It is a gift that every Christian can and should seek every day.

SIX

Responding to the Lord

THUS FAR WE HAVE DISCUSSED the significance of word gifts for charismatic prayer groups and we have discussed the five most prominent of these gifts. Now we will turn our attention to some of the practical ways of applying what the Lord says through word gifts to the spiritual life we share with the other members of our prayer groups.

When we seek manifestation of the word gifts, we must do so with the proper motivation. Word gifts are but one part of a life of intimate, daily contact with God. We should be constantly seeking to deepen our relationship with the Lord by worshipping him, by making time for personal prayer, by participating in various forms of group prayer, by reading the Bible and other spiritual material, by serving God's people in practical ways, and by seeking the word gifts.

God works in us through all these things. And each is an important aspect of our daily lives as Christians.

Just as we must be willing to seek God in all these ways, we must be willing to do what he says when he speaks a word to us. It is easy to say "yes, Lord" when the prophetic word calls us to love and worship the Lord. It is somewhat harder to say "yes, Lord" to a word about repentance or about reconciling ourselves with people with whom we have had a falling out. It is even harder to say "yes, Lord" when the Lord tells us to submit ourselves to some authority when we've been accustomed to being an independent group or when he rebukes us for failing to follow up on something he told us before.

These latter cases are sometimes called "hard words." This is because often they are hard to do. It is not easy to ask someone to forgive me, for example. But if the Lord tells me to do it, I must do it. Similarly, it might not be easy to submit my prayer group to the authority of my pastor, but if the Lord tells me to do it, I must do it. I know that each of these are "hard words" because the Lord spoke each of these words to me and they were two of the hardest things I ever had to do. But, I had told God that I was willing to do whatever he told me and I had no choice but to obey the clear word of God.

Of course, before any specific action is taken in response to a word gift, the message must be properly discerned. The elements involved in discernment were discussed earlier, in our treatment of prophecy. Briefly, they include consistent, clear repetition of the message over a period of time; reception of the message by reliable members of the prayer group; confirmation through other word gifts; and seeking guidance from responsible leaders.

To explain better how this discernment works, I will describe the process the prayer group I was part of went through in selecting and training leaders. When our prayer group was first formed, we who started it, three couples and two religious sisters, were the leaders. This was the case because we were the people with the vision for a prayer group and we were the ones committed to attending all the meetings and doing the other things necessary to build a prayer group.

Later, as new, committed members joined our group and as the different gifts and abilities among our original "core group" became apparent, we made some changes. Some of the original core group members withdrew from leadership and other people were invited to join the core group. This was more of a common sense decision than a response to a word from the Lord, but he blessed us, I believe, with the appropriate wisdom.

After some time we learned how to function as a prayer group and we learned the very important lesson about word gifts that I discussed earlier. It was time to apply what we had learned to the practical areas of leadership, teaching, pastoral care and service. Leadership was the first area to be dealt with because it is so basic and because it was our greatest weakness. We had also received comments from prayer group members about problems with our leadership.

We began to seek the Lord's wisdom by having special meetings for core group members. The purpose was to hear the word of the Lord through word gifts in the context of worship. We met for about two hours every Monday night to worship God, to seek manifestation of word gifts, and to discuss what we believed we heard the Lord saying. Afterwards, we had a brief time of fellowship and refreshments.

The Lord did speak to us during those meetings. He did not give us a specific, point-by-point plan detailing how we should proceed. Rather, he spoke to us first about how much he loved us, then about how he was with us always, then about faithfulness to him and the work he had entrusted to us, and finally about submissiveness to those he had appointed to guide us.

We had the foresight to plan to continue these meetings as long as was necessary for us to hear God's word and to act on it. As it turned out, one message built upon another until, after two months or so, we heard a consistent message. What it boiled down to was three things: listen to and watch for the needs expressed by our brothers and sisters in the prayer group, obtain guidance from leaders with more experience and more wisdom than ourselves, and continue meeting together as leaders to hear God's word and to build our relationship with one another.

These three practical steps may seem like matters of common sense now, but to a group of people very young in the Lord they were indeed wisdom from on high. And they carried even more weight because we knew they were the word of the Lord to us. We had experienced them over a period of time during which the Lord spoke to us through scripture, prophecy, interpretation of tongues and the other word gifts.

After we heard and understood God's word to us, we had to obey it in practical ways. First of all we had to consult our brothers and sisters in the prayer group. Then, we had to talk with our pastor and find our who were the "other men" the Lord had told us were able to guide us. We also had to renew our commitment to an additional weekly meeting and to an occasional leaders retreat so we could continue to hear God's word and make practical plans to carry this word out.

Some of these things were hard to do. I was not too happy with the idea of consulting our pastor. He was a man involved in many things and he had little understanding of the charismatic renewal. He was also opposed to the idea of lay people using the Bible for anything other than prayer. He had publicly stated that no one could understand the Bible without long courses in a college-level theology program. But God had told us to consult with him and, regardless of how hard this was for me, I had to do it. (It actually turned out to be less of a traumatic encounter than I had expected. Our pastor gave us a few warnings about "fundamentalism" and "elitism" and then gave us his approval to continue using parish facilities and advertising our prayer meetings in parish publications.)

Other leaders in our group also had difficulty understanding what the Lord had told us to do. Some of them eventually had to leave leadership positions. But we who stayed with it were able to seek practical wisdom from other leaders. We did this primarily by reading books and magazine articles written by the well-known and successful charismatic renewal leaders and also by attending conferences. As we began to apply what we heard, a practical plan for our group emerged. Once this plan was formulated, affirmed by the members of the prayer group, and implemented, we were ready to deal with the other important areas in a similar fashion.

This story is offered as an example of how one group of Christians tried to faithfully respond to the challenges of building a prayer group. We made many mistakes, of course. But we stayed with a basic game plan that is essential for any group of Christians who are serious about doing what God wants them to do: we earnestly sought the word of the Lord through word gifts, we made sure to discern them properly, we submitted these words to those in authority over us, and, we obeyed the word of the Lord.

St. Paul gives us two very important guidelines for proper use of word gifts. These are found in the 13th and 14th chapters of the first letter to the Corinthians and are part of the treatment of spiritual gifts which St. Paul begins in 1 Cor. 12, where we find the basic list of charismatic gifts we have been discussing.

The first of these guidelines is to use the gifts in love. This is the whole point of 1 Cor. 13, the "love passage" of St. Paul. This passage is so often read at weddings and in other contexts that its original meaning in relation to word gifts is often misunderstood. St. Paul's purpose in writing these words about love was to explain to the Corinthians and to us, their heirs in the faith, that word gifts are given to help us grow in love for our Lord and our brothers and sisters.

Paul ends the 12th chapter by encouraging the Christian people to be faithful in using the gifts they've been given and to "set your hearts on the greater gifts" (1 Cor. 12:31). The greatest of these greater gifts is, of course, love of the brothers and sisters. "Now I will show you the way which surpasses all the others," he writes, and continues with the famous description of the qualities of one who truly loves.

St. Paul's purpose in writing these words was to zero in more specifically on the instruction he gave in the preceding section, chapter 12, where he explains how the Christian community is a body and spiritual gifts are given for the building of that body. In chapter 13 he explains how Christians should use the gifts to promote love. Envy, jealousy, disharmony or any other kind of conflict is out of place in the use of spiritual gifts.

One good way to test word gifts is to apply the qualities of love listed in verses 4-7 to the message. Ask yourself "Is this message given with a patient and kind attitude? Did it come from a spirit of jealousy, snobbishness or anger? Does it rejoice in the truth of Jesus Christ? Does it promote forebearance, trust and hope? Does it encourage people to endure in the spiritual race?"

I remember an occasion several years ago when a woman gave what she considered to be a prophecy, but she delivered it at a time and in a manner completely inappropriate.

The place was Sacred Heart Church; the occasion was the Holy Thursday Mass commemorating the Last Supper. Shortly after Mass began the doors of the church opened and in rushed this woman. She "prophesied" an exhortation about people turning their hearts to the Lord, accepting Jesus into their lives, repenting of sin, and receiving the gift of the Holy Spirit.

The message the woman delivered was a very basic Christian message and I have no doubt that the majority of the people in the church that night would have benefited, under different circumstances, from the message. But, obviously, the woman was out of order presenting a "prophecy" in the middle of Mass, and the word was presented in a manner which objectively violated just about every item in Paul's list of characteristics of love. The woman seemed to be filled with anger; she was impatient and the delivery of her message was harsh and abrasive. Patience, kindness, and forebearance could not be discerned. Rather, the whole episode upset the people trying to worship God at Holy Thursday Mass. This was clearly not a word gift delivered to promote love, trust and hope among God's people.

The second guideline for using the gifts is to observe some simple rules of order. "When you assemble, one has a psalm, another some instruction to give, still another a revelation to share; one speaks in a tongue, another interprets. All well and good, so long as everything is done with a constructive purpose.....You can all speak your prophecies, but one by one, so that all may be instructed and encouraged. The spirits of the prophets are under the prophets' control, since God is a God, not of confusion, but of peace" (1 Cor. 14:26-33).

What St. Paul is saying here is to respect the rules of order when you meet. Everyone who has a word from the Lord will be permitted to speak it out, but it must be done peacefully, one at a time, with a certain amount of silence here and there to let the messages sink into the hearts of those present.

The verse about the spirit of the prophets being under the prophets' control refers to self-control. One doesn't need to blurt out the message the moment the Lord puts it on the mind of that person. Rather, the message is to be given at an appropriate time during the meeting.

Far from stifling the Spirit of God and his gifts, these simple rules of order enable the God of peace to speak to his people in a way they can understand and remember.

Many prayer groups have adopted the practice of having an experienced leader speak with anyone who believes they have a word gift to share during a prayer meeting. This is a practical exercise of the gift of discernment and serves to bring order to the flow of word gifts in a prayer meeting. Here is how it usually works:

At the beginning of the time of worship the prayer meeting leader announces the name of the person to whom word gifts should be brought. He explains that all word gifts—scripture sharings, prophecies and other sharings—should be submitted to this person for discernment. Sometimes this person may decide that a particular word is not to be shared at this meeting, and the person with the message should submit to his judgment joyfully and return to his seat. But usually the word gift discerner simply works with the prayer meeting leader to make certain the word gifts are shared in proper order with sufficient time between them for reflection and worship of the Lord who speaks to his people.

This type of discernment of word gifts is usually only done by large prayer groups. Smaller groups—those with less than 100 people—do not usually have as much need for such organization. But all prayer groups can benefit from another common practice—recording word gifts.

Some prayer group leaders tape record all word gifts and teachings so that members can listen to them again and again. This also enables those who were absent to hear the words of the Lord as originally presented rather than having to rely on other on other people's recollections. Leaders should be careful about how widely these tapes are distributed. It would probably not be a good idea to circulate them outside the prayer group because these messages are intended for the members of the particular group and may be confusing to others.

Another practice common among prayer groups is to enter summaries of each word gift in a notebook after each meeting so that the leaders can refer to them while planning teachings and other activities.

This notebook method helps leaders see the "big picture" of God's word to the group over a period of time. It might even be helpful to try to categorize the messages. For example, the words of encouragement might be kept together in one section of a notebook, the words of correction in another, the revelational words in another, and so on. This exercise can help sharpen the focus of the Lord's word in each of these particular areas.

Word gifts which are particularly significant should be allowed to take root in the lives of prayer group members by frequent repetition of the message in teachings, sharings and exhortations.

The group I now belong to recently had such a significant word from the Lord. The Lord told us through word gifts that many of us were not correctly using the spiritual gifts he had given us. We were not, the Lord said, fully using the power he had put at our disposal to bring others to a saving knowledge of him. This corrective word was delivered to us in the form of a very graphic vision and was confirmed by prophecies and scripture passages which other brothers and sisters had received.

For weeks afterwards our leaders brought our attention back to this word by referring to it at the beginning of prayer meetings, by asking people to share how they were responding to the word in their own lives, and by praying for further guidance from the Lord on how we could respond to this important word.

This kind of emphasis and practical application of the word of God is important for all prayer groups. Without it we run the risk of being only hearers of the word and not doers. Our prayer meetings then become little more than another kind of devotion; and our brothers and sisters are denied the privilege of serving God in the way he wishes to be served.

Word gifts can bear a great deal of fruit when they are delivered with the proper motivation, when love of the brethren and order in the assembly are respected, and when a vision for action emerges from them. Every member of the prayer group has a responsibility to make certain that these scriptural principles for the exercise of word gifts are obeyed.

Leaders have a particular responsibility to encourage the use of spiritual gifts and to make certain these gifts are fulfilling the purposes intended for them by God. One good way to do this is to study the gifts in greater detail. This book serves as an introduction to word gifts. On the next pages are listed books and magazine articles which provide more good information about word gifts and practical conclusions drawn from them.

One last and very important word about word gifts. God has already revealed to us the basic doctrines of the Christian faith. The particular church that an individual Christian belongs to interprets these doctrines, and members of that church should hold fast to them. Word gifts in prayer meetings are not intended to reveal new doctrines or to call into question doctrines held by particular churches. Any message a person receives that seems to be out of harmony with either scripture or the doctrines of the church that person belongs to is probably not an authentic word gift and should be treated accordingly.

Suggested Readings

Books

Cavnar, Jim, *Participating in Prayer Meetings*, Ann Arbor, Servant Books, 1974. Parts of this valuable little book deal with the operation of word gifts in the prayer meeting.

Clark, Steve, *Baptized in the Spirit and Spiritual Gifts*, Ann Arbor, Servant Books, 1976. This book contains an authoritative description of each of St. Paul's gifts of the Holy Spirit.

Gee, Donald, *Concerning Spiritual Gifts*, Springfield, Mo., Gospel Publishing House. This book is now out of print but it can be found in some libraries. It contains a description of each of the Pauline spiritual gifts and several good chapters on uses of the gifts.

Ghezzi, Bert and John Blattner, eds., *Prayer Group Workshop*, Ann Arbor, Servant Books, 1979. This collection of articles from *New Covenant* magazine contains short articles on prayer meetings and discernment of prophecy.

Ranaghan, Kevin and Dorothy, *Catholic Pentecostals Today*, South Bend, Ind., Charismatic Renewal Services, 1983. Contains a description of each of the gifts of the Holy Spirit.

Sullivan, Francis A., *Charisms and Charismatic Renewal: A Biblical and Theological Study*, Ann Arbor, Servant Books, 1982. Contains a scholar's point of view on the spiritual gifts. A valuable follow-up to the work of Clark and Gee.

Yocum, Bruce, *Prophecy: Exercising the Prophetic Gifts of the Spirit in the Church Today*, Ann Arbor, Servant Books, 1976. A comprehensive treatment of the gift of prophecy and the role of the prophet in the prayer group and the larger body of Christ.

Articles

The following articles have appeared in *New Covenant* magazine, a magazine of the Catholic Charismatic Renewal, published in Ann Arbor, Michigan.

Anderson, Paul. "Toys, Trophies or Tools." June 1981, p. 7. How spiritual gifts enable Christians to cooperate with God's grace and build his kingdom.

Cavnar, Nick. "A Place for Prophecy." February 1982, p. 4. A discussion of the gift of prophecy as experienced today.

Forrest, Thomas. "Tongues—A Gift of Roses." July 1981, p. 15. Some of the things Fr. Forrest says about receiving the gift of tongues apply to other gifts as well.

Forrest, Thomas. "How the Gifts Are Lost." October 1982, p. 15. Reflections on why some groups lose the manifestation of the gifts and what to do about it.

Jacobs, Sam. "Growing in the Spiritual Gifts." June 1983, p. 12. How to seek the manifestation of spiritual gifts.

Jungkuntz, Ted. "Optional Extras?" December 1981, p. 18. An exhortation to use the gifts God has given.

Scanlan, Michael. "Simplicity and Power." June 1981, p. 11. A discussion of the power of the gift of prophecy.

Notes

Chapter Two

1. Gee, Donald. *Concerning Spiritual Gifts*. Gospel Publishing House. pp. 27-34. Clark, Stephen. *Baptized in the Spirit and Spiritual Gifts*. Servant Publications. pp. 112-115.

Chapter Three

1. Yocum, Bruce. *Prophecy*. Servant Publications. pp. 32-33.
2. Ibid. p. 48.
3. Ibid. p. 56.

Chapter Four

1. This prophecy was delivered at the National Catholic Charismatic Conference at the University of Notre Dame in 1982. It was published in the July-August issue of *New Covenant* magazine.
2. This prophecy was delivered at the 1976 National Conference at Notre Dame. It was published in the February 1978 issue of *New Covenant*.

Other Books of Interest from Servant Publications

Spiritual Warfare
Recognizing and Overcoming the
Work of Evil Spirits
Michael Harper
One of the best books available for providing Christians with guidance about the nature of our spiritual struggle. Exposes the methods of evil spirits and provides scriptural direction for dealing with them once they are detected. $4.95

Charisms and Charismatic Renewal
A Biblical and Theological Study
Francis A. Sullivan, S.J.
An important, thorough assessment of the renewal movement that is changing the Church. For those who want to know more about the history of this dynamic movement, its theological and scriptural base, its present impact on the church, and its probable future course. $8.50

Available at your Christian bookstore or from:
Servant Book Express • Dept. 209
P.O. Box 7455 • Ann Arbor, Michigan 48107
Please include payment plus 5%
($.75 minimum) for postage.
*Send for our FREE catalog of Christian books,
music, and cassettes.*